PRISONS FOR PROFIT

What you need to Know!

ANTWAN 'ANT' BANK$

VIP INK Publishing Group, Inc.
Atlanta, GA.

Printed in the USA

Cover art designed by SK7.

Published: 7-15-2015

Isbn – 978-0-9861-340-9-8

Library of Congress Cataloging-in- Publication Data

2015944737

ANTWAN 'ANT' BANK$

1. African American Men 2. Private Prisons 3. Law Enforcement 4.Justice System

Growing up as an African-American, Hispanic or even a poor Caucasian in America is a challenge. The system is built to keep you in the lower class and it has its reasons. Billions of tax dollars are shelled out every year on food stamps, welfare, housing and many other Government assistant programs.

Even if the beneficiaries of the above wanted to become productive citizens in their own neighborhoods and make it on their own, they would be hard pressed. The local education system as well as the local economy just simply can-not or will not support its people, so other measures need to be put in place! Some will find the fortitude to get into college and or leave their destitute neighborhoods to become productive citizens, employee's, business owners, etc. But that dream is few and in between.

This environment almost always leads to the same impoverished cycle or for many, a life of crime. With no role models, local businesses or community programs around or Father figures in many of the homes; the streets usually find a way to take over.

These circumstances are more common than we would like to

admit. Many people will turn to the drug trade; some will become thieves, prostitutes, pimps, killers and drug attics. The harsh reality of your family starving with-out lights or water will make any sane person do what they need to in order to survive. Compounded with the stress of everyday poverty stricken life, hardcore criminals will emerge with a burning desire to succeed. Whether they take the legitimate route or illegal is the question.

In the culmination of it all, I can assure you that no matter what the decision; someone will be profiting from these inequalities and in that majority will be the private prisons of America. A collective of legal Corporations who soul survival is to put warm bodies in cold cells to meet a Government contracted quota. Because of this need, Government has no incentive to help these low income communities but to watch them falter instead; it's actually cheaper for them to pay Private Prisons than to invest in these communities. Giving way to an abundant prison population that serves as the modern day slave trade.

Dedicated to those who have fallen victim to poverty, injustice, oppression, crime and the Private Prisons of America.

ANTWAN 'ANT' BANK$

PRISONS FOR PROFIT

What you need to Know!

VIP INK Publishing Group, Inc.
Atlanta, GA.

Table of Contents

1

Perfect Prey

As infants, raised in low income housing your child will be exposed to the perils of everyday life. They will watch you struggle to make ends meet from day to day. A single parent home is normal for them and most of those around your neighborhood. As they get a little older they will start to admire the neighborhood kid that has both parents at home, if that even exist.

Playing with their friends every day is all that's on their

minds until that day comes in head-start when all of the neighborhood kids are in one room together. It is here as humans where they will all begin to bond. Every personality in the room will mimic what they see at home. The teacher will become appalled at some of the things she/he sees or even hear. During this point your child will be identified as a good or bad kid.

From here on an open dialogue should be on going with the parents and teacher. Your child's life and future will depend on it. Sadly to say but this can also be the first time a behavioral record would be kept on your child. This document will eventually end up being a disciplinary report that will follow them throughout the school system. It is detrimental that you take control of the situation at this point. If your child is acting out this is the time to correct it. Once they start kindergarten they will be exposed to more peers with attitudes and behavioral problems.

At this age kids are monitored by counselors to see how they will function in society. It is your job as a parent to mold them into respectable, caring human beings. If you don't, the school system will do it for you and their way is to write down and monitor all activity. This will determine if your child needs behavioral medication, mental counseling, remedial-schooling, advanced schooling or even considered a genius.

As a parent you have the power to mold your child's mind to be successful, so you must do your part. Not doing so will leave them for the wolves that are waiting on the streets, in prisons, county jails and juvenile detention centers. You must understand that the environment your child grows up in will influence their minds. This includes TV,

Movies, Media, Home, Neighborhood, Music and School.

The reality is that too many of us parents allow the streets and depend on a poor school system to raise our kids. Many School's under educate due to lack of Government funding in poor communities and most of the time Schools don't even have enough teachers because they can't afford their salaries.

Be conscious that during the progression of schooling that their disciplinary records can and will eventually transcend into arrest records that will lead to juvenile hall then into career criminals if you're not on top of things. Collectively it can create the perfect storm for a life of crime and fat pockets for the private prisons. You may not want to believe me but this is no accident!

Once your child becomes a teen with a disciplinary school record whose been brought up with a poor education, lack of parenting, moral support and behavioral issues he/she will revert to the human trait of survival by any means necessary. Eventually they fall victim to what they see on the streets every-day, be it selling drugs, robbing banks, stealing cars, clothes, jewelry, the sex trade, etc. They will want the American dream and the only way that they will know how to get it will be through crime.

So the same cops that watched them grow up and walk to school every-day, the same cops that spoke to you about what your child did in school, that same cop that patrols your neighborhood knows your child by name as well as their disciplinary school record and he will be the one taking them away.

The Government doesn't give a damn, so it's up to you and the other parents to create a community that Educates, supports and promotes positive role models in your environment. It is your responsibility to take trips away from the neighborhood with your child and explore other things, expose them to other opportunities and people. If you stimulate a child mentally and show them what the world has to offer they will aspire to be so much more.

You must remove that inferior complex that government assistance has instilled in the community; i.e. Low income housing, food stamps and welfare does not have to be a way of life! When they're at an age where they can make the choice to change and break that poverty cycle you must empower them to do so instead of teaching how to live off the system. Every parent should teach their children the value of free enterprise. You will be amazed at how creative they can be.

2

The Hunter

In a report by – Thinkprogress.org it stated "the United States has the largest prison population in the world. More than 2.4 million people are inmates; over half that number consist of inmates with drug crime sentences for 1 year or more."

Of the incarcerated, black men are 6 times more likely than white men to be in prison, Hispanic men are 2.4 times more likely. The FBI has estimated that 1 in 3 Americans have a criminal record.

The (ACLU) American Civil Liberties Union reports that "America with only %5 of the world's population has %25 of the world's prison population. We are the world's largest jailer! 1 in every 99 adults are living behind bars, 1 in every 31 adults are under some form of correctional control, counting prison, jail, parole and probation population."

Private Prisons – A place which individuals are physically confined or interned by a company that is contracted by a government agency. These companies enter into contractual agreements with governments that send them prisoners to house. The government in turn pay the prison's an agreed amount each day or per month for housing that inmate.

This practice started in the south at the end of slavery when plantations and businessmen needed to find replacements for their freed slaves. In 1868 they started leasing convicts from prisons to supplement their workforce. This continued well into the early 20th century.

Once America declared a war on drugs the prison population began to become overwhelming, many facilities were over-crowded and the states and federal government couldn't afford the cost. This being America, private businessmen saw an opportunity where they could move from leasing inmates to do cheap labor to owning the prisons and so it begun.

The 1st private prison business; (CCA) Corrections Corporation of America emerged in 1984. The company secured its first government contract when it was awarded full control of a prison in Hamilton County,

Tennessee. More private prison businesses would follow.

As of 2013 the United States Department of Justice stats show that 133,000 state and federal prisoners were housed in private prisons. Below is more information on these companies that you as American citizens should know.

CCA *(Corrections Corporation of America)*

1. Owns or Manages private prisons and detention centers. Holds contracts with federal, state and local governments.

2. Is the largest Private corrections company in the U.S.A

3. Manages over 67 facilities and owns 92,500 beds.

4. Founded by Tom Beasley, Robert Crants and T. Don Hutto. These businessmen had extensive experience in government and corrections prior to forming CCA.

5. Based in Nashville, Tenn.

6. Revenue: $1.73 Billion dollars

7. New York Stock Exchange call letters. NYSE: (CXW)

8. Industry: Private Prisons (Adult, Juvenile, Immigration)
9. "In 2012, CCA sent a letter to prison officials in 48 states, offering to buy prisons from these states in exchange for a 20-year management contract and a guaranteed occupancy rate of %90."

GEO *(G4S Secure Solutions)*

1. Industry: Outsourced Correctional Services.
2. Organized as a Real Estate Investment Trust.
3. Specializing in Corrections, Detention and Mental Health Treatment.
4. Operates in North America, Australia, South Africa and U.K.
5. Founded by George Zoley
6. Head Quarters: Boca Raton, Florida.
7. In 2005 acquired Correctional Services Corporation for $62 Million, 2010 acquired

Cornell Companies for $730 million.
8. Revenue: $1.61 Billion
9. New York Stock Exchange call letters. NYSE: (GEO)

CEC *(Community Education Center)*

1. Specializing in Private Jails and Halfway Houses.
2. Operates in 17 American States and Bermuda.
3. Manages 14 jails, 26 halfway houses aka Residential Reentry Facilities.
4. Based in West Caldwell, NJ.
5. Even though its employees have been charged numerous times with smuggling drugs to its inmates the company still retains its state, city and county contracts.

Note: Let's hypothetically say that the Government pays CCA $1 a month for every bed that they own. CCA currently owns 92,500 inmate beds in the United States. That equates to $92,500.00 month, multiply that by 12 and you get $1,110,000.00 a year. Now put yourself in the position of the CCA and tell me what lengths you wouldn't go to in order to occupy those beds.

This hypothetical is only based on $1. Realistically it's more like $100 to $500 a day per inmate. Any businessman worth their salt would come up with all kind of incentives to meet these quotas! So now take a look at what role the Media, Music Business, Schools, Poverty, TV, Movies and Laws that require stiff drug sentences play in the scheme of it all. It's simple supply and demand! There's a demand to fill the beds in Private Prisons and certain areas all across America are designed to supply the product! *(African American and Hispanic Males make up the majority)*

Community Service

Community Service is simply a trade-off. You will work off your debt to society for the crime you committed. It usually comes with other stipulations like, drug and alcohol test, curfew or some kind of rehabilitation classes. You may not be physically behind bars but you're still incarcerated in the system. The outcome can be good or bad depending on how you adjust.

Probation

While on probation you will be monitored like a kid. Depending on the level of probation, you may have to urinate in a cup every week, call in everyday at a certain time, wear an ankle monitor, be in the house at a certain time and hold a steady job. Being employed in itself is a feat for a convict or felon.

This is where your biggest challenge will come. How to find a decent paying job with a criminal record and knowing that you will be violating your parole or probation if you don't have one! The judicial system is designed to fail those that fall victim to it and society plays right along.

The pressure and obstacles you will face with a criminal record often leads back to a life of crime. Not because you don't want to do better but because you are now and always will be labeled a criminal and nothing will or can, change that. It will follow you until you die. The judicial system doesn't care if the crime you committed was an accident or even if it happened 20 years ago. In the eyes of the law and Society you don't deserve the same opportunities as a citizen without a criminal record. Now can you see how supply and demand is continuously met to fill these beds in these Private Prisons? *(It's a Trap!)*

Small Town Economy

The average small town in rural America has a weak economy. Those that are prospering are often doing so because of a strong farming industry, industrial plants, factory warehouses, etc. But all of these towns are not so lucky. Many have opted to participate in adopting Private Prisons to boost their struggling economy. The more inmates a prison holds, the more jobs it can offer to that economy. Prison's has indeed become big business in rural America parallel to those factories, warehouses and plants.

In this setting the Prison becomes the catalyst to the town's very existence. Hotels, Restaurants, Entertainment, Shopping centers, etc. will all exist to appease the citizens, employees, inmate visitors and other industries that will contract the inmates from the Prison's for cheap labor.

Again I say; any businessman or woman worth their salt will do what needs to be done to keep their business revenue flowing. It just so happen that the product of choice is criminals and systems are in place to keep that product coming. Open your eyes and look at the big picture! America is a Business and Private Prisons is just another Corporation at the table.

Poor Education

When you don't have knowledge of something or don't understand it; to you it doesn't exist. You must feed your mind as much as you can so that mentally you can remove yourself from an undesirable situation. It is through these thoughts that you will manifest your dreams into existence.

Here's some knowledge for you. Say you spend $30 a month on cigarettes. You stress everyday about where the next dollar is coming from, you're living off government assistance and you have a child on the way, the baby is due next week. So that day comes and you and your family are all in the hospital greeting the new family member. A friend of the family who sells insurance walks over to you, ask if you want to come to his office next week and speak about purchasing some insurance products for your new borne.

You look at him like he's crazy and tell him to stop tripping; my baby just got here and how could he think about your baby dying! But what you didn't know is that if you had taken the time to purchase an 18-20 year insurance investment product for your baby, you would be paying less than $30 a month for those 18-20 years for a 1 Million dollar product. Then when your child turn 18 you could have withdrawn some money from the value of that insurance product to buy your child a car and paid their way through college or help them start a business. I know you heard of that saying. "A trust fund baby"! Well there you have it!

Because you didn't know about how that insurance could have helped your child, that scenario didn't exist to you. As parents you should explore the unfamiliar when it comes to educating your child. Look at successful people and find out what they're doing then make it work on your behalf.

I heard my Mother say once that an idle mind is the devils tool shop. That stuck with me and I can tell you that my mind is never idle. If you don't have much right now, educate yourself by reading, listening and watching empowering, informative and inspirational people then aspire to be just like them. We are all made of the same energy; anything is possible!

You must take yourself to where you want to be mentally

first then the physical will follow. Without this you will fall victim to your negative surroundings and you will relive what you see and hear. Now if you're surrounded by positive influences and energy than the same is true and that's where you want to be.

One can become educated outside of the School walls, you will be surprised! By instilling this character in yourself it will be passed on to your children through your actions. Each one, teach one; education doesn't end and begin in our School systems.

Justice System

I'll be the first to tell you that the Justice System isn't about much Justice at all. It's flawed to a huge degree. Yes in some cases it has proven to be right in its decision but the same can be said for the many times that it has failed all of us tremendously. It is controlled by man and anything controlled by man can and will be corrupted.

Unfortunately the only way that you can assure that your child does not fall victim to the long arm of the law is to keep them away from it and that's damn near impossible. The horrible truth is that they can fall victim to it at any-time or any day. I look at the system as a huge dark cave with a big entrance way and the only way out is through this little red door all the way at the other end of the cave and it's locked.

Once you're in it, they (Government) want to keep you in it. If they let everyone out how could the beast survive? So they put you on probation, incarcerate you, put you on house arrest, you do your time for the crime but after you've paid your debt to society the charge still follows you for the rest of your life. That damn sure isn't rehabilitation it's Bullshit!

A felon has no choice but to become a career criminal unless there's someone around to influence, educate and mentor them. Show them the few options that they have left, not even a college degree will erase that criminal charge off of their record. The deck is stacked and cemented together.

This is why you must educate your kids and teach them to dream. The odds were never in their favor. It's up to you to turn the tables.

The Police

I have several friends that I grew up with that are now police officers and I spoke candid with them about their jobs and the way they uphold the law. Based on what they told me, in my opinion there is too much of a grey area.

Officers are allowed to use their own judgment when dealing with too many scenarios. It's never cut and dry, there is always something to weigh their decision. It can be race, attitude, peer pressure, quota, money, etc. Leaving this kind of power in an officer's hands is dangerous. It's really not fair to any of us if you ask me. You can be speeding on your way to work, get pulled over and given a ticket by one officer on Monday.

You can speed down that same street on Wednesday in route to work, get pulled by a different officer and given a warning when you actually told him the same thing you told the other officer "I'm late to work!" But you broke the law in both cases. In the eyes of the law both officers would be right. Now how is that Justice?

This should bring awareness to the fact that the same methods are being used in your neighborhoods and on every corner. One officer can choose to warn, discipline and provide other options for kids that they see selling drugs, stealing, etc. while the other will arrest them every time. Believe me! It happens and I know some of you have seen it too.

This is a dangerous game and many times it leads to police officers thinking that they're judge and jury. Many officers fall victim to the God complex. Some try to be upstanding and go by the book but some-times even they falter.

Police officers have become the bad guys in our society. Too many minorities fall victim to their brutality resulting in death, false imprisonment, harassment, profiling, etc. Only a small percentage of the officers have been guilty of this but that's all it takes.

They have lost our trust and most importantly our youth no longer fear or respect them. This combination only adds to an already impoverished society of under privilege youth. When they don't respect the cops or even fear prison, we have a problem. As parents we can't allow them to fall prey to the justice system or as I call it, TRAP!

Teach your kids to study the cops and their behavior. You must make them aware of the power these officers have and how they can use it to change lives. Most of the time this isn't for the better; Police come when they're called. They exist to fight crime and keep order by reacting to a response. Think about it! How many officers do you know that will voluntary knock on your door then say "Hello Ms. Jones, I'm here to protect you today, I'll be sitting right here on your porch, making sure no one comes to bother you."

It doesn't happen! Unfortunately, police are a necessary evil, not a welcome Angel.

The Media

Anyone reading this book is familiar with the voice and faces for Allstate, the NBA players that advertise with State Farm. The Attorney's radio jingle that you hear every morning while driving in your car on the way to work, the lizard or cave men for Geico, Flo for Progressive, you get the point!

Radio, TV, Newspaper, Blogs, Social Media, Yahoo and Aol home pages, Billboards and Magazines. These are all mediums that use its platform to fight for your attention, your mind, your money, your life! Marketing Executives spend countless hours on ad campaigns to grab your attention visually, physically, sub-consciously, etc.

The same strategy is used to brainwash our kids into the criminal system. Radio stations only play music that celebrates negative images like Murder, Drug dealing, Alcohol abuse, infidelity and more. Reality TV has compounded the crisis with distasteful images of minority women.

Whenever your child listens to this music or watch TV, they're doing it at a repetitive rate. After a while they start believing what they see and hear. They become desensitize to the negativity.

This in turn subconsciously becomes a part of their everyday behavior. Lyrics of popular songs that are being played on the radio, over and over every hour becomes the premises to their daily life routine. "In the kitchen water whippin" (Making Crack) Young ladies aspiring to be trap queens and like the shows on TV they aspire to be side chicks; ie. *"Scandal" "Being Mary Jane"*

"Empire" promotes how the entire inferior, poverty, drug infested neighborhoods can be used as a platform to make it to the top. The whole back story is a familiar one that we as a minority people are trying to move on from but how can we when radio and TV that's controlled by the majority promotes it as being ok!

All of the above is aligned to create the perfect prey to keep the Government contracted beds filled in those private prisons. Wake up people, it's a business and this is the part you call supply and demand! The Media desensitizes illegal acts therefore our kids start to believe that smoking weed, selling drugs, etc. is ok because if it wasn't, it wouldn't be glorified on the radio, TV and Movie screens. Now would it?

The same can be said for homosexuality. Yes some people really do identify themselves as homosexuals naturally but the way the media throws it in your face and glorifies it. Our kids think it's a choice, like it's the newest style or something. Parents take control of your kids and guide

them the right way or they will
be lost.

3

Economy

An impoverished community equals self-destruction for our youth. In a situation such as this, parents must make it their business to stay involved in the everyday routine of their child's life and also hold them accountable.

If your kid is not able to find work or isn't old enough to work yet, please find an extra-curricular activity to occupy their time! Sports, Church functions, Community centers like the Boys and Girls Club, YMCA, etc. can play a big part in your children's future.

The alternative is boredom which will eventually lead to mischief in some form or another. Whether individual or with a group, this is never good. It is in this forum that the habits of criminal behavior will sow its seed.

Like I stated earlier when it comes to law enforcement; the officers never come unless something or someone shines light on a crime or situation. In other words the police force is one that reacts and is mostly never pro-active. Once they're made aware of a potential crime or threat it's their duty to respond. The same goes for a Detective working a case. Once they're assigned to that case their job is to close it. Hence the reason their reaction is always like a Pit Bull attacking a wounded dear. They are trained that way whether the attack is physical, mental or investigative. It's their job!

I use the analogy of a Pit Bull because once their jaws are locked on your kids. It will take a damn good attorney, a lot of luck, money, Family, community and Self Advocacy to free them from the jaws of the Justice System!

Unfortunately the battle has proven to be too much for the average parents living in these poverty stricken, under educated, inferior neighborhoods that continuously serve as a hot bed for career criminals that almost, always will find themselves sleeping in the private prisons that our Government will pay to house them instead of building up the endangered community to curve the problem.

This is the same Government that's quick to garnish our

paychecks if we don't pay our taxes. You must understand that most minorities have been relegated to the lives they live now.

Because of this some illegal acts has become the biggest commodity in the neighborhood. It forces our youth into a life of crime by necessity not by choice. Factor in no available jobs, no community support, a poor education, and being dependent on welfare, food stamps and section 8 housing; this in itself enables oppression.

Government assistance is a temporary tool that should be

used while you as parents are trying to make a better life for you and your family. If your child grows up in this system and all the chaos that it enables, they too may keep repeating the same process.

It's all a trap and I'll keep saying this because I believe it to be true! Think about a caged animal that you feed and shelter every-day. Pretty soon that animal is going to get tired of that same water, bread and cage he's been trapped in for years.

He can see the free animals running wild on the outside of his cage, eating and drinking what they want. They come and go as they please. He wants the same but doesn't have the knowledge to unlock then walk away from his cage. So he keeps eating and drinking until anxiety gets the best of him. He bites, pulls and kicks on the cage door until it comes open.

Now free, he has to find a way to eat and shelter himself. After being caged, fed and under educated for years he lacks the knowledge of hunting and finding shelter. He looks back at the cage then turns around and gaze at the green grass, other animals and trees that surround him.

Admiration to be free takes over so he gallops in the direction of the other animals eating their catch of the day. Aggressively he growls as he approaches then charges for the neck of his now opponent. Caught off guard the opposition falls in defeat as the former caged animal runs away with his dinner.

Little did he know that in some walks of life, what he just did was considered a crime! First was vandalism; Second assault, third robbery. The need to be free activated his survival mode without knowing the consequences of his actions he simply took what he wanted.

As humans we share that same trait, in fact many of us are successful because of it. The problem is that more of us need to teach our kids the difference between the right and wrong approach. We must do this if we want to keep our youth out of those prisons.

Lacking in jobs, community programs, education and government funding equals more money for prisons and that's the bottom line. In my book "**Gate Key**: *Turning your High School Education into Millions*" I provide several ways out of this rat trap. If you want a brighter future for you and your kids this book can help tremendously!

4

The Game

We all are granted a certain amount of time here on earth. It is what you do with this time that matters. Falling victim to poverty, crime, government assistance and an inferior education will deprive you of the opportunity to be great.

A child that is born into these circumstances is already 4 steps behind in the game of life. Parents in order for you to change these odds you must first take accountability then recognize what part you play in this. Your children will end up in the same position for their entire life unless you take the necessary steps to change their future.

Giving your child instruction on the game of life while their still young will enable them with a huge advantage! You should always respect their minds and speak to them like intelligent adults, even at the age of 5 and 6 or even younger. You want to be able to hold a meaningful conversation with them at an early age. By doing this you challenge their minds which will only be training them for the future.

Take time to teach them common sense. Like how to read people and the situations that they will inevitably find themselves in. It may not sound like much but believe me this teaching will save you from that dreaded phone call that you don't want at 4:00 am in the morning.

Having the peace of mind from knowing you've had that talk will open the talk path to more powerful and knowledgeable conversations. You want your child to have the ability to hold an intriguing discussion with any elder.

Coaching them on how to read people and their actions will challenge their minds to analyze any situation and or opportunity, good or bad that will present it-self to them. This will become evident when they come home and sit down with you to discuss how they avoided a bad decision just by listening, observing and walking away from an individual or bad situation.

As adults we've all made mistakes. These mistakes are great teaching tools as long as you're candid with your child when discussing them. You can truly show them how one decision controlled the outcome of your life, be it positive or negative.

The challenge is to keep them on the right side of the law. This however can be truly difficult if you find yourself in a crime riddled community. It's your duty as a parent to implement the skills, mind set and knowledge to make them successful. Set aside some time to enlighten them about becoming entrepreneurs and what dreaming is all about because this will not effectively be taught in their school.

Your challenge sits outside of your door every day! Youth that are less fortunate are running in a rat trap trying to survive. Without the necessary skills from you they will do what's needed to make it.

In an impoverished community the majority of things that surround you exist because of negative energy derived from poverty. Drug dealers, Prostitutes, Drug attics, Thieves, Gangs, Robbers, Pimps and Murders are so prevalent until they seem to be a legal career choice.

When in fact they are the same variables that will make your child's life more valuable to a corporation of private prisons that will get paid from our

Government for giving them a bed in their facility. If your child ventures down this path they will more than likely be labeled a felon or career criminal forever!

This will only make it hard for them to become successful at anything but crime in the future. This is why you must understand the game of life and insulate it in them so that they do not end up in this Trap! Show them the BIG picture. (*A Black or Hispanic male's life is worth more in prison than it is on the street!*)(*And it won't be the Black or Hispanic males cashing in either!*)

5

Disadvantages

Children must be exposed to other options besides what they see in their communities every day. The same can be said for teenagers and adults. The thought of knowing that something different even exist outside of their world is priceless. Parents you should teach the meaning of free will to your kids at an early age and constantly challenge them to think outside of the box.

Assure them that any and everything is possible. Parents must create a support system that respects their children's choices. This is not to say let them do the wrong thing but instead let them have the choice to decide wrong or write and reward or discipline them accordingly.

The biggest disadvantage today in households is that too many children think that they have the advantage when it comes to discipline. They want to call social services or even the police when they get punished. Society has given way, to a soft approach; unlike back in the day when parents were strict. More parents fear jail now when it's time to punish kids. This behavior has led to more juvenile delinquents than one could even imagine.

As if to say! "Don't spank or punish your child let the law do that for you!" The law and social services forgot to mention that they have a nice cold cement bed waiting on them though! And the Government is going to pay to keep them fed and clothed too!

It is very important that we recognize our surroundings and how it affects our lives and the choices we make. The human body and mind is amazing; it will adapt and overcome any situation but the power lies in the decision one will make during these opportune moments.

When it comes to the perception of minority men and women there usually is always a preconceived notion. One should take this disadvantage and use it to their advantage. Empower yourself and let the so call elite think what they want all while listening to their preconceived notions then take your position when they least expect.

For the most positive outcome there has to be a role model or mentor in place. Without either many teenagers will become vulnerable to the long arms of the law. Sadly there isn't many of each in the impoverished communities and illegal acts many times become easy choices.

In a perfect world every child would grow up with great role models, two parent households, a great education and success beyond measures. But that isn't the case because many fall victim to poverty, crime and neglected societies. The perfect balance of those negative variables creates a sturdy platform for what will become career criminals and meal tickets for many private prison corporations.

6

Convict

Children that find themselves with a continuous inadequate disciplinary school record will more than likely transform that behavior into adult hood where the corrective action is no longer in-school suspension, study hall or expulsion but incarceration.

If this behavior is not rectified at an early age by their parent, an adult, mentor, role model or community program or leader; a criminal career path may very well lay ahead. This book is not meant to scare you but to educate, inform and empower with the knowledge, skill set and motivation to keep yourself, your kid, family member or friend on the straight and narrow.

Jails and prisons are not built to educate and rehabilitate but are used to fill community man hours with free or cheap labor from inmates and is also used to fill contracted man hours as well for contracted corporations. Breaking the law is how you get there!

As a prisoner one will give up their right to vote amongst other things. Your criminal record will hinder you from a good paying career which will make it that much more difficult to stay on the right side of the law once you are released.

You will forever be labeled a convict and or felon. In most of the cases that land you in prison or jail, too many inmates will leave those four walls with a felony or misdemeanor on their records. It's important to know that this will remain on your record forever unless you made some kind of deal with the District Attorney during trial or your deal to have it removed once your time is completed. ***"Forever"*** *let that soak in!*

It doesn't matter who you are this will affect your confidence, self-esteem and way of life. This pressure can force you to turn to the only option that you believe you have. *"The life of a Convict"* *"A career Criminal"!* It will take strong will power, a great game plan, education, luck and an unwavering focus to stay on the straight and narrow.

7

How to get out!

Convicts, felons or criminals on the way back to society must adjust their way of thinking. One must focus like an entrepreneur from this point on. The way that society is set up, most employers require a background check and this will reveal any criminal records which dims many chances when it comes to most job opportunities.

Focusing on a future through the eyes of a CEO or business owner will motivate said person to create ways to legally survive by being their own boss. The drive to succeed from past failures will either motivate to do the right thing or the wrong to survive. At this point it's up to the individual to take self-advocacy.

Education is still an option but it must be chosen wisely. Even still the focus of a business owner should drive this decision. Studying to be a Doctor, Lawyer, Dentist, Chiropractor, Hair Stylist, etc. are some professions that a convict, criminal or felon can acquire and be in charge without answering to any employer that requires a background check.

Ones environment can make it very easy to fall into the long arms of the law and its corrupt justice system. Black and Hispanic men are an endangered species. Poverty even now is still on the rise, prisons are benefiting from our ignorance, our woman are becoming more educated than men because more of them are in school while men are behind bars and the media along with the music, movie and television business use their platform to promote the negative stereo types.

This keeps a constant flow of the wrong things in the public eye while our kids believe the lie! *"It's ok to do this!" "Look you can go to jail for 10 years, get out and still become rich!" "You can sell drugs too!" "Prison is cool!"*

The truth of the matter is that all of it manufactures the perfect criminal! It's up to us to change because everyone else including the government is in it for the money.

"Prison beds for dollars!"

Thank you for reading Prisons for Profit. I truly hope that it will make a difference in your life. Don't hesitate to leave a review on my Amazon or Barnes & Noble comment forums. I would love to hear from you! If you want to contact me directly, you may do so via Printhousebooks.com

Other titles available from this Bestselling Author:

Amazon Bestselling Trilogy

The MADE; Crime Thriller Trilogy is about Andy Cooper; a military vet, turned hustler, turned Gangster, turned Crime Boss. His marriage is on the rocks; fresh out of the military, AC finds himself broke and lost with a Wife and three kids to feed. Trapped in Sin City and working any job he can get from day to day, to make ends meet. Hating the state of mind he's in right now, a really fucked up way to be! Gone are the days when Uncle Sam paid for housing, day care and groceries. Now, all own his own again, with no idea of where life is going to take him. One thing for sure, Andy "AC" Cooper no longer wanted to wear that Army uniform another day. Coop loved every minute of it and would not trade it for the world but the next chapter of his life was about to start. It just so happen that he landed in Las Vegas, one of the hardest cities to make it in, it is truly the land of the Hustler. What the outsiders don't know is that beneath the bright neon lights, the delicious buffets and luxurious casino's, lays a whole different world that would eventually suck him in.

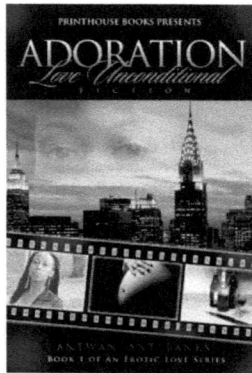

The word Adoration can be defined as fervent and devoted love or simply put; to worship. During our time on Earth we will all experience this powerful thing called Love. This novel will take you on a journey seen through the eyes of four couples and their relationships. For Love we endure amazing things and some of us will go to the limit to keep it.

Love can fill your heart with joy or leave it filled with hate. Adoration explores love at several levels; some of them good; some bad. In Book One of this Series; hearts will break, tears will fall, blood will shed and bells will chime; all in the name of love.

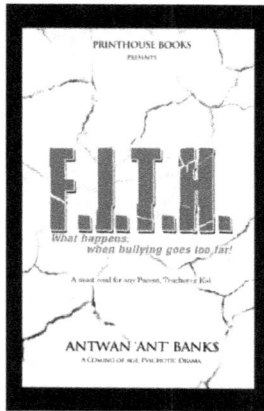

F.I.T.H. is a Drama about a High School Freshman and a Bully. The situation becomes very intense when the bully doesn't let up. Although the victim tries his best to have tolerance and handle him accordingly, no matter what he tries, nothing seems to work. After several run-ins and close calls, the victim is forced to become the Bully's favorite mark, influenced

by an ever presence of fear, his life as he knew it; changed.

These collection of spirits; were some of my favorites to mix for the thousands of customers that I served as a bartender back in my 20's. During 1995 - 1996, I worked as a bartender in several Las Vegas Clubs and had a damn good time doing it! I've included a few recipes I picked up from fellow bartenders, some from customers and most I've learned from bartending school.

Mixology is an art and if mastered one can make a really good living serving spirits and conversing with the people you serve at your bar. If you're a bartender looking for some new drinks or you're just someone interested in mixing up some new drinks in your kitchen. This book of spirits is for you. Welcome to the Party Life and remember to drink responsibly.

Miss Jones, Book 1 of Series.

The Cover Girl series is about, an Atlanta; Eye Candy photographer; name Malakhi Jones. Pronounced (Mal uh Ky). This short story and many others to come; will take you inside a day in the life of a hot photographer and his daily encounters with several of the industries sexiest Magazine Models and Video Vixens.

While these events are Fiction; anyone in the industry knows; what goes on at the shoot; stays at the shoot! Malakhi is at the top of his game and he's connected with every

Men's Magazine Publisher, Casting Directors, Hip Hop Artist and Talent Managers in the industry. Getting a session with him is like winning the lottery; when it comes to being an eye candy Model, in the ATL. Any Model knows; that once the session starts and that camera flashes; all rules will be broken to obtain that success; if not! Then keep dreaming.

In book 2 of The Cover Girl Series: Lola Love. Malakhi ventures on an on location shoot, with the Sexy Chocolate, Video Vixen; Lola Love. Her enticing aura almost proves to be too much for the A List Photographer but in true Malakhi fashion; he prevails. The two meet up, downtown on Peachtree street Atlanta; at one of the Cities five star hotels.

Together, they will create magic for the camera and hot lustful memories in their Jacuzzi Suite. They say a picture is worth a thousand words but only the photographer and the model knows; what exactly goes on, between those poses.

In book 3 of the Erotic Cover Girl Series: Madam Grace. *Malakhi encounters the lovely mixed beauty Madam Grace. While handling business as usual he soon finds out that this beauty has a kinky side. The photographer however is always up to the challenge and Grace proves to be that and some.*

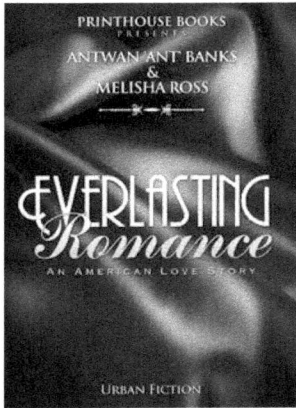

From the backdrop of the ATL; the hottest city in the South, comes a compelling love story about several friends and their adventures in College at the A.U and their professional careers while in the city of Atlanta. Experience Love, Drama, infidelity and historic memories as you indulge yourself in this Romantic tale of fiction. Set in 2001-2002,

you're sure to reminisce back when Jay-Z, Nelly, Luda, Missy, 112, Lil Jon, Alicia Keys and more were in heavy rotation on your favorite radio station. When T.I's album; I'm Serious had the city crazy, the clubs closed late and Ying Yang had those ATL Shake stages rocking and dollars raining.

Everlasting Romance, An American Love Story explores the essence of friendships, life, Love and how those bonds molded several individuals into a close knit family while in the hot city of Atlanta. Donnie, Quentin, Chantel, Cynthia and their friends; found themselves sharing love at every level; Brotherly, Sisterly and most of all intimately! But; at what cost!

PRINTHOUSE BOOKS

ANTWAN "ANT" BANKS

In the City of Atlanta; the Gentlemen's Club Industry reign Supreme. Along-side the fledging music industry that contributes platinum hits every other month, together they both pull in Billions of dollars each year. You would actually have to live here or frequent the ATL to see the marriage these two have committed to each other.

The biggest misconception is for

someone to assume that it's all illegal. What many don't know, is that the city of Atlanta benefits off of every Stripper, Bouncer, Waitress, Dj and Bartender that works in the Gentlemen Club Industry. The truth of the matter is, for any girl wanting to Strip here in the ATL clubs, such as Onyx, Majic, Strokers, Pin Ups, Shooter, Follies, Blue Fame, Blaze, Oasis, Cheetah, Pleasers, Diamonds, Babes to name a few, and trust me there many more! You must first have a permit, from the County that club is in, before you can even think about dancing on any stage in this city.

Yep that's right! These permits can only be obtained from the County Sheriff Department where they perform a thorough background check for Felonies and any open Warrants. If you have a conflicting felony you *will not get a permit! If you have a warrant, you will not be leaving through the front door but going to the back in handcuffs instead. Permits range from $250-$475 per year depending on which club you are getting a permit for (That's every-year!). How do I know, you ask! Well, let's just say when I first got to the A, I took a Doorman position at one of the most notorious clubs in Atlanta where I met thousands of dancers whom led me to write this story. The club shall remain anonymous because they fired my butt for hustling too hard; Hell I was just trying to show them how to get paper. After all, I did just close a club back in South Khak that I ran for 12 years. Anyway that's another   story.*

Regardless of what you may have seen or heard, the competition in these clubs are fierce and that makes for some slow nights when it come to the cash flow for some girls. So some of them, more times than none; take it to the next level and do what they like to call private parties. For you squares out there, that means Escorting or Tricking if you want to keep it street.

I found myself in an interesting position while working at this ATL Gentlemen's club. The dancers confided in me and asked me to be their driver to some of these so called private parties. The stories from those nights and from other private discussions we had while riding in my car, was unreal! My true passion and God given talent is a writer, so I had to ask these girls if I could tell some of their stories; while keeping them anonymous of course. I was happy as a Kid in a candy store when they agreed. So here it is; several accounts of the ATL night life through the eyes of many dancers that I rolled into one character, whom I named Tahiry. Laced with Cocaine, Molly, Weed, Lean and Z-Bars, this life is in no way, full of glitz and glamour, true crime rides along at every turn, from the streets of ATL this is our story, cold Hearted and Street Official. R.I.P to the dancers we lost to the Strip Hustle. We got love for you.

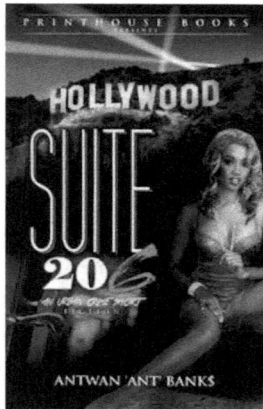

Millions travel to the City of Angel's every year in search of that one shot at stardom. But most fail and find themselves caught in the underbelly with the homeless, the drug attics, prostitutes, thieves and murders. Candy and Joe unfortunately are no different than most and end up living in a different hotel every other night; doing whatever needs to be done just to survive.

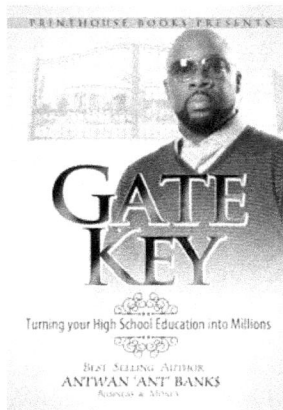

Gate Key: Turning your High School Education Into Millions *attacks the glue that holds the very fabric of the higher learning institutions together. It gives hope to teens that find themselves in despair. It creates opportunity for those in lower class society who seem to be destined for a life of poverty and unemployment. It turns that one way street to becoming a criminal into an 8-lane highway of self-preservation.*

Gate Key will not only spark the flame to ignite the inner fire that we call a dream. It reveals over 30 lucrative professions that can be started while in high school or immediately after which will place our youth on a road to success without the need for a college education.

The awful truth is that only 4 out of every 7 teenagers will go on to attend college after graduating high school and for many reasons some will not complete this journey. Everyone wants the American dream for their kids; they want them to get a degree, find a great job, get married and have children, buy a house with a white picket fence then live happily ever after. Here's a shocker! The American dream will be just that for many of our youth, a dream! Too often teens can't afford college, have no interest in going, did not prepare for it, have kids early or are undecided any one of which causes them not to attend college and to head straight into the sub-par job market. Minimum wage can barely pay utility bills let alone take care of a family; this, more times than not, places our kids in the lowest class of society (in reference to a three-tier society of Lower Class, Middle Class or the Upper Class).

This book gives our youth a choice as to what class they want to end up in, how much income they want to earn and how to begin that journey while still in high school without getting any student loans or attending any college. It will put our youth on track to become prosperous entrepreneurs and professionals by making them aware of career choices that they probably didn't even know existed for them as teens.

*Gate Key doesn't only make our youth aware of these opportunities, but will show when, where and how to start one of these featured career paths while still a teen. This book is designed to open doors for those that cannot or will not be attending college after high school for some reason or another. Even now you have the power in you to be whoever you want to be! My purpose is to open your eyes to some of the many options that the world has to offer. After all, it was said best by our forefathers in **The Declaration of Independence**:*

"We hold these truths to be self-evident, that all men are created equal, that they are endowed by their Creator with certain unalienable Rights, that among

these are Life, Liberty and the pursuit of Happiness"

PRINTHOUSE BOOKS.

Read it, Enjoy it, Tell a friend.

VIP INK Publishing Group, Incorporated.

Atlanta, GA.

www.PrintHouseBooks.com